It's All About
WHAT YOU
MAKE IT

VALERIE CHEELY

outskirtspress

DENVER, COLORADO

Table of Contents

Foreword

"It's All About What You Make It" - truer words could not have been spoken. In marriage as in life, what we contribute to the mix determines the outcome. This must-read guide, testament and instructional book encourages the readers to be accountable and responsible to their marriage vows, their mate and ultimately to themselves. This simplistic script belies the profound and brilliant message that will strengthen a struggling marriage, give momentum to a mediocre marriage and add an electric spark to an exceptional marriage.

No matter how good your marriage is, it can always be better. It is time to raise the bar in your marital relationship. "It's All About What You Make It" challenges you to do just that. Complacency is a deadly venom to any marriage. The antithesis to complacency in a marriage is attention and work, work and attention. If no kindle is added to the fire, the fire goes out. If the wrong kindle is added to the fire it will smother and go out. This book gives the readers good kindle that will help ignite the fires of passion, excitement and caring to their marriage. It also leads one to acknowledge that it takes the spirit, cooperation and determination of both partners.

Ager and Valerie Cheely are a unique couple with an uncanny ability to "make things work" when life's obstacles persist. They have discovered the value of teamwork, single mindedness and intentional cooperation in a relationship. They do not claim to have the "perfect relationship" and are not exempt from life's obstructions inside and outside of the marital vows. What they have discovered and what has made their marriage so successful is their determination to fulfill the scripture that declares "and the two shall become one flesh. So they are no longer two, but one flesh." (Mark 10:8) They understand that therein lies the secret to a triumphant marriage and that this is an everyday test/task - nothing occurs by happenstance. The beauty of their quest is that it has become so engrafted in their being that they want to share it with others.

This book should be read by couples contemplating marriage, the newly married or those married with seniority. Take to heart the golden words, loving advice, encouraging examples and challenging instructions. The "take away" is that whatever state you find your marriage in, it can always be better. It is all up to you - what you make it. A victorious marriage involves hard work, sacrifices, and self-denial, but the payoff is matchless.

Acknowledgement

Our commendation and congratulation to Ager and Val for caring enough to share out of the depths of their hearts wisdom of their understanding. Their abiding faith in God, devotion to the principles of His Word and determination to walk in His Will has led them to enjoy the pleasure of each other and the blissfulness of marriage. We pray that the boldness that is imbedded in this print will serve as a beginning, guide, stabilizer or enhancer to your marriage.

A True Blessing to anyone who reads this book!
Pastor Micheal and First Lady Y'Vonne Benton
Fairfield Baptist Church, Lithonia, GA

Preface

This book is dedicated to our family and friends that have shown so much love and support during this life-changing transition. I thank God for blessing me with this vision to write a book to encourage, inspire, and motivate married couples. I am humbled by the experience and honored that God has entrusted me to deliver this message to his people. I am grateful to have been blessed with a husband who is my business partner, best friend, everything you can ask for in a husband, and the co-author of this book. Our life together along with our two children, Adonis and Aniya, our precious gifts from God, has been a faith journey, and a true testament to "It's all about what you make it" and we've made it the absolute best!

Introduction

Many times in marriage we want to find the ideal solution, resolution, or conclusion to the problems that we encounter. We want that one perfect way to solve it all, to keep things alive, and hope that issues never arise at all. The reality is, problems will come, but we don't have to allow them to determine our end. We have to know that it's all about what we make it. We can choose to allow the problem to destroy our marriage, or we can choose to destroy the problem. As husband and wife, how you handle situations will not be the same in most cases because men and women typically think and process information totally different. It's not so important how you get to the resolution, what's important is that you get one that works best for you both. It takes two to make a marriage work. It takes telling the truth and being able to take the truth to have open communication in a marriage. It also takes two trusting and believing in God to be able to stand the test of time.

It's all about what you make it and you have to focus

on what works best for the two of you! Often times we compare our marriages to other couples, compare our spouses to other people, and find ourselves wishing that our relationship could be like someone else's. The reality is, it can't and won't ever be exactly like someone else's marriage. You're not them! God's plan for them does not fit you. As the old saying goes, "Get what you get and don't pitch a fit!" You have to make the best of what you have. The person you chose to marry, chose to marry you. You made that choice and you had a reason for making it. Now you have to decide how to make the absolute best of it! Although in marriage, you go on dates, the reality is, it's no longer the dating game. Marriage is real and should be for as long as you both shall live. So, how do you make it last? It's all about what *you* make it!

A relationship/marriage has to be designed just for the two people that are in it. Honesty and trust must be a top priority in the marriage along with open communication. This will create a strong foundation and lead to a long lasting winning marriage. It's important to recognize, release, and resolve individual issues and find faith and forgiveness to bring freedom into your marriage. This makes it easy to love, entice a yearning to make love, and create the desire to show love. It's all about what you make it and how much time you're willing to put into it to make it work. You must put God first and allow him to show you the way and the work becomes easier because you're allowing God to lead you and you're using the word of God as your guide.

In marriage, couples must always put God first! Putting God first in your relationship requires "Triple A". That is acknowledging, accepting, and appreciating! Acknowledging must first start with reverence to God as the head of your house. Proverbs 3:5–6 says, "trust in the Lord with all thy heart and lean not to your own understanding. In all thy ways acknowledge him, and he shall direct your path" (KJV). Therefore, you must first acknowledge God in every aspect of your marriage and believe that the word of God is the ultimate guide to a successful, long lasting relationship. And even when things in your relationship seems lost or simply going down the wrong path, Matthew 20:11 says, "For the Son of man is come to save that which is lost" (KJV). So Acknowledging God will keep you through the better and the worse, guide you, and direct you to the right path that God has designed for the two of you. It does not matter if you see a situation or circumstance that has happened in your marriage as bad, acknowledging God gives you confidence and assurance that things can and will work out. Romans 8:28 says, "And we know that all things work together for good to them that love God, to them who are the called according to his purpose" (KJV). Your marriage has a purpose that's been designed by God, and it will work out just the way you want it to, if you acknowledge God and allow him to show you the way!

God's word gives us the direction, instruction, and correction that we need. Therefore, we have to accept every part of it to get what we need from day to day. To accept God's word, you have to accept Jesus as your personal savior and be open and willing to allow his perfect will to be done in your life. And the Word of God instructs us to love the Lord thy God with all our heart, all our soul and all our strength. And to do that, you have to accept him. And Romans 5:8 says, "but God commendeth his love towards us, in that, while we were yet sinners, Christ died for us" (KJV); which tells us that God unconditionally accepts us. Therefore regardless of what is going on in your marriage, God will help you. You have to be willing to accept His will both individually and as a couple. God will accept you just the way you are and implant his change agent into your heart, so that you can accept your spouse for who they are, and start to love and appreciate them even more. Being married is a privilege, and a gift from God that isn't necessarily granted to everyone; so accept God's will and thank him for trusting you to be a part of his ministry of marriage.

In everything, give thanks! Appreciation comes from the gratitude and thankfulness that God loves you so much that he created a mate just for you. Your appreciation is shown from the things that you do. You have to show God your appreciation for your marriage first by doing what the word of God instructs you to do as a husband and as a wife; then giving thanks to God for His love, protection, and the provisions that he gives to you every day of your life. Tomorrow is not promised, so you have to show appreciation today. Ask your spouse, "How can I show you that I love and appreciate you today?"

Although marriage is made up of two people, the husband and wife, "Triple A" (Acknowledging, Accepting, and Appreciating) must be applied individually as well. It is hard to acknowledge, accept, and appreciate someone else if you don't apply it to yourself first. Acknowledge your feelings and why you feel the way you do. Good or bad, share your feelings, so that they can be addressed. It has to be acknowledged that your spouse has feelings too. And when you feel that things need to change or be different, you have to accept the things you cannot change, know that God has given you the ability to change the things that you can, and he will give you the wisdom to know the difference (The Serenity Prayer). Accept who you are. Accept when you need to change. Accept who God has called you to be. So often we try to change our partner, and only God can do that. When there's a change that's needed, the first order of business is yourself. Ask God to transform your mind to accept your spouse for who they are, love them, pray for them, and thank them for being who they are in your life. There is a reason, a purpose, for God allowing the two of you to join together as one. You have to pray, ask God; then trust and believe that he will show you what that purpose is. Jeremiah 29:11 says, "For I know the plans that I have for you, says the Lord, thoughts of peace, and not of evil, to give you an expected end" (KJV). He knows the plan and He is the source to all that you need to fulfill your purpose in your marriage. Even when you get to a place of not knowing and there's uncertainty as to whether or not you are the husband or wife that God has ordained for you to be, rest assure that when you seek God, you will be able to acknowledge, accept, and appreciate who you are. Once you know, accept it, and you will see things so differently in your relationship and start to acknowledge, accept, and appreciate your spouse for who they are!

Chapter One

"Two to Tango!"

"Two to Tango!"

You can dance alone, but it's much better with a partner!
And you can't tango, if only one of you want to dance.

"God's principles for marriage have not changed. Husbands are to commit to their God-given authority to provide, protect, and to love. Wives are to help their husbands and submit to their God directed leadership. Husbands and wives have to be truly committed to God's program and design because if it is ignored, division within or of the marriage is the result. We can seek to redefine God's plan according to our own desires, but ultimately human wisdom cannot compete with the all wise God"! (1) It's important to understand that the design and plan for marriage was for two people, a man and a woman. In Genesis 2:18, it says, "The Lord God said, it is not good that the man should be alone; I will make him an help meet for him" (KJV). The Word continues in verse 22, "And the rib, which the Lord God had taken from man, made he a woman, and brought her unto the man" (KJV). "God making woman from the man's flesh and bones illustrates for us that in marriage, man and woman symbolically become one flesh. This is the mystical union of the couple's hearts and lives coming together." (1) God's plan for marriage is for these two people to come together as one. Genesis 2:24 reminds us that, "Therefore shall a man leave his father and his mother, and shall cleave unto his wife: and they shall be one flesh" (KJV) also see Matthew 19:6.

It takes two to tango relates to the fact that it takes two people in a marriage working together to make it a success. Throughout the Bible, God treats this special partnership seriously. The goal should be more than friendship, it should be oneness (1). Marriage is like the tango, not the electric slide. In an article called Tango: A Deeper Look, there are many aspects of doing the dance tango that relates to marriage. When you look at how the tango is described, it symbolically helps to define how the marriage partnership should work. Its intimate embrace and intertwining of two people can be exciting and irresistible for some, yet scary and intimidating for others (2). The key is, you can't dance to the beat of your own drum. You and your dance partner have to be listening to the same music. Husbands and wives have to be on one accord to move in the same direction in their marriage.

Tango is described as being sensual, romantic, and intimate (2). The same applies to marriage, the continued focus on putting God first, along with the disciplines of prayer, partnership, and protection will keep your marriage moving in the right direction. The moment you lose focus on God's original plan for marriage, it can be perceived as being too difficult to continue on. There must be daily strategies in place to cultivate your marriage and establish family routines. Putting the right disciplines in place will also allow your marriage to be the tango that it was designed to be. It will keep the two on one accord; moving in the same direction and to the same beat!

And the two shall become one..........And the oneness starts with prayer. Prayer has to be priority and your spouse should be your #1 prayer partner. Couples that pray together stay together. When you pray together and for each other, you want to be on one accord. We often pray and ask for our wants and our desires and forget to ask what God's will and desire is for us. How often do you pray and meditate to just listen and hear from God so you will know what to prayer for. It may sound funny, but prayer is a two way communication; there is a time to speak but more importantly, there should be time to be open and ready to listen.

We assume that we know what our spouse needs and wants without even asking! Are you praying for God's plan for the both of you or is everything you ask for camouflaged by your own wants and desires that may not even line up with God's will for your marriage? When was the last time, you asked your spouse his/her prayer request? Have you asked them what they are praying for or petitioning God for on your behalf and on behalf of the family? Try this, just take a moment to hold your spouse and talk about your prayer request and then pray together! Praying together allows you to hear the heart of your spouse; to hear them openly make their request known to God and to you, and there's no guessing. It should not feel uncomfortable. It should feel like dancing to the same beat; moving in sync' and not stepping on each other's feet. God will honor the unity that he has ordained for two people coming together on one accord to make their request known to Him as a unit; standing on His promise given in Matthew 18:20 which says, "for where two or three are gathered together in my name, there I am in the midst of them"(KJV). Putting God first and praying with your partner will give you peace, patience, and power to solve any problem and push forward to a prosperous marriage.

Partnership is an important aspect in marriage. You can dance alone, but it's much better with a partner. And you can't tango if only one of you want to dance. *Tango: A Deeper Look* also tells us that tango is improvised one step at a time, so partners must remain attentive; responding to one another continuously. This is important to stay on beat and move in sync. Dancers adjust the embrace as needed to keep the channel of communication open, allowing every step to serve the spatial and musical unfolding of the dance. There has to be adjustments in marriage. You have to be open to suggestions and feedback on the next moves to make in your marriage to create a good partnership. You have to be willing to listen to your spouse and continuously pray for a clear understanding of the needs of your partner. Partnership is about working together to accomplish a task. In marriage the task is maintaining a healthy and happy relationship that's designed for partnership, not isolation; for intimacy, not loneliness.

Protection in your marriage helps to maintain the wholeness of each individual as they grow physically, mentally, emotionally, and spiritually within the oneness of the marriage. Ecclesiastes 4:9-12 says, "Two are better than one because they have a good reward for their labor. For if they fall, the one will lift up his fellow, but woe to him that is alone when he falls, for he have not another to help him up. Again if two lie together, then they have heat; but how can one be warm alone? And if one prevails against him, two shall withstand him, and a threefold cord is not easily broken."(KJV) The responsibility is for both the husband and the wife to protect each other. The protection extends to every aspect of their well-being. With constant prayer and putting God first, the spiritual aspect is protected. With creating a partnership and ensuring their opinion and input matters, protects the mental and emotional aspects. And making your partner feel comfortable, desired, and wanted, provides the physical protection of the marriage. With that being said, you both have to want your marriage and be willing to do whatever it takes to protect it. It is impossible for one person to make a marriage work.

It's like dipping yourself when you tango, you are sure to hit the floor. You need your partner to catch you and stand strong with you. You want your partner to feel confident and secure, not insufficient and as if something is wrong with them. When you provide protection, it ensures the love and respect that's needed in marriage to hold up the principles it was designed for.

It takes two to tango! It takes two to be in a marriage! The old school hip-hop rapper, Rob Base sums it up best, "It takes two to make a thing go right, it takes two to make it out of sight"! Prayer, Partnership, and Protection are the right disciplines to keep your marriage flowing as two people dancing to the same beat, moving in the same direction, and moving to the motions of what God purposed and designed for marriage to be!

Chapter Two

"Tag Team"

"Tag Team"

Knowing your role in your marriage is very important, and being confident in your role is crucial when it comes to working together as a team. Yes, in a marriage, you're either a husband or a wife. However, there may be times when you have to switch from your typical role and take on other responsibilities that are usually done by your spouse. There's no magic trick to identify when this needs to happen, you have to be in tune with what's going on in your home. And you have to know when the switch needs to happen. As a wife, there may be situations that require you to have strength like a man, and think like a man. As a husband, there may be circumstances and situations that make you emotional, require you to show emotion, and expect you to feel emotions like a woman. Does that change who you are? Does it change the God given responsibilities that you committed to? No! It's just "tag you're it"! It's your turn to take on that particular task, duty, or responsibility.

T.A.G. breaks down to

- T---Telling your partner when you need help.
- A---Accepting how they handle the situation or duty.
- G--- Giving them credit for taking on a responsibility that's out of their comfort zone. It's about both people Taking, Accepting, and Giving. Often times rather than tagging our spouse we become frustrated and/or upset, and it usually results in a heated discussion that has nothing to do with the situation at hand.

To T.A.G.team is all about the interchanging of words, work, and willingness. You have to be in tune with when it's time for you to tag. So as a team you have to establish expectations on what to say and how to say it. You have be clear about what it is that you actually need or want help with, and be willing to do whatever it takes to achieve more together. Words are important, but putting them into action makes the difference.

To T.A.G. with words can be easy and hard at the same time. The words are easy; just hard to come out. T is telling your spouse when you need help, however sometimes it is hard to explain what it is that you need or want help with. We have to be careful not to blame our spouse because we can't explain to them what we need. And carefully choosing our words is very important because one word can change the meaning of an entire sentence, and could be detrimental to the effort altogether. You have to be sure to recognize that both roles are important and you cannot demean what the other person does. It's so easy to speak negatively or say the wrong thing when you're frustrated or angry with your spouse. And so many times we say things that we truly regret saying later, and it's hard to fix it. That's when it's time to play tag you're it! You have to be willing to figure out a way to make this situation okay, and figure out the right words to say.

With words there are some do's and don'ts. Tag the do's and take away the don'ts to get rid of the negative, and make the positive a habit. Do compromise— Don't complain. Do communicate with confidence---Don't close up and coward down. Do create—Don't compare. Do come together---Don't control. Do compliment--Don't curse and condemn. Do confess when you're wrong---don't contradict and count mistakes; Count how much you care, and be considerate! Do have compassion---. Don't command. Do call and connect and count until your calm- Don't come home late and angry! Do concentrate on the present and commit to the future together and making your marriage last--- Don't constantly bring up the past!

It takes work to T.A.G Team and you have to be ready when it is your turn. Most homes are organized with roles and responsibilities that each person is assigned to take. Whether you have a large family or a small one, to Tag Team the responsibilities makes things so much easier and prevents your spouse from getting O.F.F.—which is Overwhelmed, Frustrated, and Fatigued! You become overwhelmed because you feel like there's so much to do. You become frustrated because you feel like you don't have enough time or help to do it. And you become fatigued and so tired that you can't get it done or don't want to do it! To Tag Team work you have to establish the expectations of the roles and duties around the house. For example the husband may cut the grass, wash the car, take out the trash; a wife may cook, wash clothes, and clean the house. No matter the task, when you are ready to T.A.G, all you have to do is ask. So turn it O.N. (Oppose the Need) to eliminate the O.F.F (Overwhelmed, Frustrated, and Fatigued)!

If you have/are a wife that is home all day, cleaning the house and getting prepared for when everyone gets home, having/being a husband who's willing to take on at least one part of that responsibility on the weekend or when time permits, will give the wife a little boost of energy to want to do even more when everyone is asleep and it is time to be alone. And yes, it can and does work both ways; it is Tag Team! You may have a husband that takes on the majority of the household responsibilities, so giving him a chance to relax will help him better relate to you and be ready to meet your needs too.

There has to be a willingness to T.A.G team. Whether its money, maintenance, or meals you have to be willing to work together to make it right and get it done. You must set, frequently revisit and discuss, and reset expectations that meet the need at the time. Things, situations, feelings, people, and circumstances do change. Whatever responsibility it is, the willingness has to extend to being reachable, agreeable, and teachable. Reachable means willing to be available when needed. It's hard to "TAG" someone who's always away, away and not answering, or simply ignoring or refusing to answer. When you are willing to be reachable, your spouse will feel more comfortable and open to telling you what the need is. To be agreeable is to be willing to do or allow something; able to accept; pleasing or pleasant. If you frequently complain about what you're asked to do, your spouse will be hesitant to "TAG". Although the task at hand may be uncomfortable to you, it's important to give it a try before saying what you won't do. Your spouse will be more pleased that you tried and pay less attention to the fact that the task may not have gotten completely done. Trying creates the right atmosphere for a teachable moment. Being teachable is being willing to allow your spouse to show you how something should be done or needs to be done. There are, of course, certain task that you do and your spouse may not have ever had to do it. However if/when that time comes, you have to allow them to show you how to get it done; especially if it's imperative that it gets done a certain way.

Good habits, consistent routines, having order, and organization makes it easier for your mate to be willing to take over when needed. Therefore planning, prioritizing, and making the right preparations are key plays in "T.A.G You're It"! Plan in advance and have arrangements in place that will make the transition easier when the tag is needed. Prioritize so your spouse will know what should be done first when they have to take on the responsibility. And good preparation is having systems in place before hand so no matter who needs to complete the task, everything is already set and ready to go.

In marriage a successful game of "T.A.G" takes teamwork. Recognize that both roles and everyone's responsibilities are important and you have to work together to ensure that everything gets done. Remember...**T. A. G**. T--- Telling your partner when you need help, A--- Accepting how they help you and handle the situation or duty and G--- Giving in and giving them credit for taking on a responsibility that's out of their comfort zone. It takes words, work, and willingness to be reachable, agreeable, and teachable so you can plan, prioritize, and prepare to do whatever it takes for the family.

Chapter Three

"Take Time Out"

"Take Time Out"

The great thing about time is, we know every day, how much of it God has assigned for the day. We know that there's twenty four hours in a day, however, we don't know what could happen the next day or even the next moment. Neither are promised, but if God gives us the opportunity to wake up another day, we need to use every second, minute, and hour that we have wisely. To better maximize this time, we have to ask God to show us the way.

Many times we take the time that we have with our spouses for granted, thinking they will always be able, alive, and available for us. Are you ready when that's not so? What happens when your spouse is not able to show you affection? When you're married you should give like it's all you got, love like it's your last moments, and laugh until you can't stop. It is important to make every moment count. Whether it is five minutes or an entire day, make it the best that it can be. Make every day great! Treat it as if the next moment is not going to happen. It's not the quantity; it's the quality that matters. Never take time for granted, and be thankful for every day God allows you the chance to wake up with your spouse, and gives you the ability to wave and say hello to your spouse, and the capability to wow and woo your spouse!

It's very important to take time out to revisit why you got married in the first place. What made you interested in your spouse? What attracted you? Ask yourself the question, "what is it about you that made me say I do?" And most of all what made you fall in love and resulted in you vowing to spend the rest of your life with them? Take time out to remember the time, reevaluate the commitment, and repeat and renew the vows; for better or worse, for richer or poorer, in sickness and in health, until death do us part. Those are words that you should forever keep in your heart. Take time out to love, listen, and laugh! Take time out to talk, touch, and say thank you. Take time out to walk together, read the word of God together, and worship God together. Take time out to plan together, play together, and pray together. Taking time out to make time will create a marriage that will win and a love that will never end.

When you love your mate, you will take time out to listen. True genuine time with no cell phones, no television, no distractions, no computers, no tablets or other electronics, just open ears, an open mind, and an open heart. Make your environment conducive for listening. Communication is one of the most important aspects of marriage. True and attentive listening allows you to respond carefully, react with caution, and reach out with compassion. It shows your spouse that you are really trying to get a clear understanding of what they are saying. So with communicating there is listening and there's talking. It's important to always say what's on your mind. You can't be focused on the grammar, or even what you feel the person speaking should say and/or how they should say it. The goal is to get it out. So what's important is that they are saying it and it's coming from the heart. When you focus on everything else, rather than taking the time to truly listen to the genuineness of what's being said, you miss the message, and you risk your spouse shutting down and not sharing again. You always want to be considerate, tactful, and respectful, but say what you need to say. Not saying what you feel allows the feelings to become like a brick. The more you hold your feelings in, the more bricks you stack. Before long, you have a brick wall! It's hard to tear down a brick wall!

Take time out to date. Realizing that the days are long and most of the time very busy, you can get so caught up in the busyness of it all, and totally forget about your mate and the time needed for the two of you to be alone. Just take a minute to call. A lunch date over the phone is better than nothing at all. Before you know it, days have passed, weeks have gone by, and even months with the way time will fly by. Dates don't have to be fancy, they can be free. It's the time that matters, not the money. So even if it's a movie night in bed, take that time to just clear your head of all the worries of the day. Hold your spouse, caress your spouse, and before you know it, movie night is over...enough said! It can be a candlelight dinner at home, no kids, just some time alone. It can be a bubble bath with some tea in the tub, some oils, a massage, or just a good body rub! It's not what you do; it's how you do it. If you know your spouse, all you have to do is put a little thought to it!

It's important to take time to make time before it's too late. Image this:

The postman ran at 4:00am this morning just to deliver a life changing message to you via mail. You wake up at 6:00am and before doing anything else, you check your mailbox; only to find one valid official letter stating that your spouse would die that same night at 9:30p.m. What would you do? In this case, the scenario presented forces your mindset to do all you can for your spouse, suddenly. Forgetting about everything else and doing everything you can in these last hours to show how much you love them; nothing is too big or too small......watch that corny movie, sit patiently while she/he shops, knock out that honey do list, cook that favorite meal that he/she likes, just simply doing everything you can to show your love and appreciation before time is up. It also puts us in the mindset to see past our spouse's imperfections and see the bigger picture. The question is, why wait for that moment......tragic news? Why wait for the unthinkable to happen before realizing the importance of taking time out to show your love each and every day. The reality is, no one knows the day nor the hour that that time could be. The fact of the matter is, we can never get time back. The arguments in the past, you could have settled, but just had to have the last say. The nights that you went to bed upset about something silly. The times when you were not considerate of your spouse's feelings are the times and things we would think about after the fact. When we really think about it, we know deep down inside that we never really meant any harm, but simply too proud to just admit our wrong and move on.

To have a healthy marriage is like having a healthy body. The better you take care of your marriage, the longer it will last and the better it will be. To care for your body you have to take time out each day to feed your body healthy foods, exercise regularly, and have regular checkups. If you don't, you see the effects that it has on your body; it creates health issues. The same thing with a marriage. You must take time to feed your marriage healthy habits. Take time out of every day to make love; take time out of your day to call; and take time out to pray, even if you don't know what to say. Create wonderful memories;

take time out to just hold each other and do nothing at all. It's ok to love hard, and with all of your heart, so take time to make time because you don't know the day nor the hour that death will do you part.

Chapter Four

"Take and Tell the Truth"

"Take and Tell the Truth"

It's time for a C.H.A.T–
couples to hear about the truth!

So many times as married couples, we say tell me the truth, but in reality, we can't take it. It's hard to tell the truth, and most of the time, we really can't handle the truth! There are three phases before finally getting to the truth of the matter. And as you continue to read, you'll recognize that you've been in or may be in one of the phases.

<u>Phase 1 of Take and Tell the Truth…</u>

This phase is made up of defensiveness, denial, and doubt. This is where your response to the truth typically starts with being defensive. For example, "I can't believe you said that!" "Do you really feel that way?" "Why haven't you said anything before now?" "That's not what I meant." "I didn't say it that way!" Or we go into denial saying, "I didn't say/do that!" "I don't act like that!" "You took that the wrong way!" Then you start to doubt, and say things like, "You don't really love me do you?" "Maybe this marriage was not meant to be." "I'm not the husband-wife you want me to be." "I just don't know what else to do."

Phase 2 of Take and Tell the Truth...

Because the responses in phase 1 are so natural, it leads to phase 2 which is fussing, fighting, and frustration. In this phase, your house is no longer filled with warmth, love, laughter, fun, and friendship; it is now a house of "intense fellowhip" that's quiet, cold, lonely, and fearful.In this phase, everything seems wrong and you've become so frustrated that you just want to be alone.

You want the truth and some resolution, but no one wants to be calm enough to stop and pray for an answer. The question is, when we get to the truth of the matter, how should we handle it? What should we do with it? How should we respond – how should we react?

The goal is to get to Phase 3 of Take and tell the Truth!

This phase consist of having faith and forgiveness to get to freedom! A simple formula to help deal with the truth is: the truth \ (faith + forgiveness) = freedom. The Bible tells us that the truth shall make us free. So in actuality, any time someone is ready to tell you the truth, you should be excited to get it. But the reality is, it's hard to hear and your responses and reactions vary. You have to recognize that how you react will dictate or determine how they will respond and it affects the outcome.

Never fear knowing the truth. No matter how bad the situation may look, the word of God reminds us in 2 Timothy 1:7-8, "For God hath not given us the spirit of fear; but of power, and of love, and of a sound mind. Be not thou therefore ashamed of the testimony of our Lord, nor of me his prisoner: but be thou partaker of the afflictions of the gospel according to the power of God" (KJV). With this assurance, you don't have to fear the situation because God has given you the strength and power to deal with it. You don't have to be ashamed because whatever you are going through is only to make you strong. God will help you overcome whatever it is so you can share your testimony; trust and believe, you are not alone. Therefore, when you have a question in your mind about any aspect of your marriage, don't be afraid to ask it. Being afraid to ask the question is the same as being afraid of knowing the truth, (the answer). When you have questions and you never ask them, it is the same as living a lie because you're not being open and honest with yourself or with your spouse. Therefore your marriage is not moving forward and this is the reason why. Yes the truth sometimes hurts, but living a lie not only hurts emotionally, it's a damnation to your soul, so it's a deeper, far worse hurt spiritually. To embrace the truth, you have to trust God with all your heart, mind, soul, and spirit and know that no matter what it looks like or sounds like, God has given you the power to deal with it. All you have to do is:

P.R.E.S.S.	P.R.E.S.S.	P.U.S.H
• Please	• Pray	• Pray
• Recognize	• Recognize/Release	• Until
• Every	• Express Your Feelings	• Something
• Situation has a	• Seek God for an Answer	• Happens
• Solution	• Save Your Marriage	

It requires pressing the hurt, pressing into the unknown, and pushing out the feelings that have been suppressed and held in for so long. When you press, press, push, that means you are ready to get it out! You're ready for an "Enema moment"! This is a cleansing within your marriage, and being freed from the hard, built up stuff that you've held inside for so long! You're getting to the truth!

There are things that we hold on to as individuals that prevent us from moving forward and being free in our relationships. It's built up so much that you have to take some drastic measures to press, press, and push it out! You have to understand and be ready for the fact that when it comes out, it can hurt, it may be messy, not look good, not smell good, and it could be all over the place. Therefore, you have to be willing to accept the mess of the truth when it comes out, and understand that it is a self-cleansing for both you and your spouse. It might be a confession, a hidden/dark secret, letting go of baggage, possibly adding some baggage, creating some pain, might leave some things hanging, and even cause some scar tissue. But once it's out, you will feel much better!

Press, press, push! Once it is out, you have to be willing to accept it, deal with it, and decide at that moment what it is that you need to do to move forward. You may have to nurse some scar tissue; but that's the process of healing. And once it is out, flush it, don't just sit there and dwell on it and allow it to continue to "stink up" your marriage. It's time to get up, "freshen up", and move on. Have you ever flushed the toilet, and then days later, what you flushed comes back up? No, that doesn't happen. It goes into the sea of forgetfulness and never returns. That's a good example for us to follow. To get to the truth of any matter, you have to conversate. Once the truth is out, you have to quickly evaluate. To move forward, and get pass this, you have to eliminate, "flush" whatever it is that has caused the issue in the first place and never bring it back up again. Trust God and thank him for the truth. He will give you the strength and wisdom to move forward and by faith he will see you through.

And that's where Faith comes in. You may not be able to see how to move forward, but the book of Hebrews

11:1 reminds us that, "now faith is the substance of things hoped for, the evidence of things not seen" (KJV). So as you take action, place your hope in God who's the author and the finisher of your faith. And no matter what the truth is or what has happened in the past, Philippians 3:13-15 says, "Brethren, I count not myself to have apprehended: but this one thing I do, forgetting those things which are behind, and reaching forth unto those things which are before, I press toward the mark for the prize of the high calling of God in Christ Jesus. Let us therefore, as many as be perfect, be thus minded: and if in anything ye be otherwise minded, God shall reveal even this unto you" (KJV). So press, press, push knowing that the truth has made you free and God has given you the faith and the freedom to move forward for your marriage to be all that you desire for it to be!!

Press + Press = Push
Truth/ (faith + forgiveness) = Freedom

Chapter Five

"Test of Time"

"Test of Time"

We said our vows! We made a commitment!
Commitment demands action
and goes hand in hand with responsibility.

Commitment is about making a choice. You know what actions you need to take within your marriage; now it's simply deciding and making the choice to actually do them. There is nothing too hard for God, so you are free to do whatever it takes to make your marriage work, have the love and unity that God has ordained, and be the husbands and wives he has called you to be. It's a lifelong adventure that requires time, work, and determination. God's plan for marriage from the beginning was for one woman and one man to commit to each other exclusively and permanently (1). So when you took the action to get married, your first choice to make was doing whatever it takes to stay married. You have to be determined to keep your commitment to your spouse and in your marriage.

It all started on your wedding day when you said I, (your name) take you to be my (wife/husband), to have and to hold from this day forward, for better or for worse for richer, for poor, in sickness and in health to love and to cherish from this day forward until death do us part! And whether it was traditional or nontraditional you made the commitment to the actions, and the times that you would choose to take the action during your marriage and for how long!

Marriage is ordained by God and when you choose to follow Christ and obey the Word of God, that's the ultimate commitment to your marriage. This commitment is symbolic of Christ and the church. When you think about the love that Christ has for the church, it's unconditional. Is your love and commitment to your spouse unconditional or is it based on what your spouse can do for you? You entered into this union vowing that only death would dissolve it; so why is it so easy to break the commitment the first sign of an issue, problem, or something going wrong. Marriage is permanent and commitment is essential to its lifelong success.

The test of time in marriage is about commitment, communication, and compromise (Triple C). Commitment involves loyalty and allegiance to God and to your mate. Communication involves honesty with yourself first, then a pledge to your mate. Compromise requires integrity, and a willingness to surrender and submit. It's not about always getting "Your Way". Triple C must partner with showing compassion, being considerate of each other's feelings, being there to comfort(be a listening ear), understand that everyone has a moment of weakness, and never stop giving compliments(everyone loves to hear how pretty/handsome they are).

So our challenge is to recommit to our spouses. Make a new commitment to your marriage with open/honest communication and a willingness to compromise. Commit to spending time, energy, and creativity to find ways to serve with

Christ-like submission. Commitment, communication, and compromise will allow your marriage to stand the test of time.

There is an A. R. T. to commitment. It takes Action, Responsibility, and Time. There is an old softball cheer that we did years ago that said, "You have to want it to win it, and we want it bad". How bad do you want your marriage? To take action to commit, you have to want it, to win it, and both people have to really want it bad, and be willing to do whatever it takes to keep the commitment. You have to be sure that your actions live up to the words. Saying I love you should be equal to showing I love you! Even God put his words into action. John 3:16 tells us, "for God so loved the world, that he gave his only begotten Son, that whosoever believeth in him should not perish, but have everlasting life" (KJV). Love and marriage has to be more than lip service. Yes we want to take time out to talk and communicate, but taking the action to show

how much we love with gestures and a touch can really mean so much more. Action is about showing love, how we respond, and how we listen; and being that shoulder to cry on. You have to make the effort to do "something" to show your love and commitment to the marriage.

Take A.C.T.I.O.N!

Actively Contribute to Touching, Intimacy, Oneness, and Needs. When you take A.C.T.I.O.N, your commitment then partners with communication and compromise. You have to talk to know what action to take and you have to be willing to give and to take to ensure both of your needs are being met. The action you take can determine how your spouse will respond from the moment you wake you until it's time to go to bed again. Why not make it really count; it's about creating a moment that you don't want to ever end. Touching and intimacy is such a huge part of marriage. They allow the mental and emotional feelings of your partner to transform into an act that creates a connection that physically shows you how your partner feels about you. And when you are confident and aware of how your partner feels, there's a sense of oneness and you become more excited and ready to meet their needs.

The true test question is, whose responsibility is it to keep the commitment? To stand the test of time, both people in the relationship have roles and responsibilities to ensure every aspect of the marriage is maintained. And that's where true compromise comes into play. Both of you looking out for each other. It's not about just making sure that "my needs" are being met; it's about the overall welfare and concern of the husband and the wife. Along with that responsibility is accountability. The vows have been made, and you are accountable to each other to ensure that each person honors their promises, to love and to cherish for better or worse, for richer or poorer, in sickness and in health, for as long as you both shall live.

The responsibility lies within the physical, making love to keep the love, the mental/emotional, giving and receiving by saying I love you, and by taking action to show it. When you think of your spouse, you should think love and feel love. Also with responsibility comes response. How do you communicate with your spouse? You are responsible for how you act and how you respond; whether it's happy times or sad times; intense fellowship or intimate fellowship. The responsibility you have in your response is to communicate clearly and truthfully. It's O.K. to ask, if you don't understand, acknowledge to show that you recognize and respect your spouse, and admit when you're wrong, didn't understand, or took something the wrong way. You both have the responsibility to hold each other accountable to that every day.

Commitment has to be there from the beginning. You have to be willing to put in the time because it may take some time to truly get to know each other. And that's ok; Marriage is for a lifetime; till death do us part. Most people don't go into a marriage thinking they're only going to be married for a few weeks; you go in knowing that you're making a life time commitment. Whether you dated a long time before you got married, or you knew each other for short time; making the decision to be fully committed to the relationship shows that you're willing to put in the time that you've vowed to as long as God allows. You're continuously finding out new things about yourself as individuals which can change the dynamics of what you originally committed to, so as you grow, the more you know, and you have to gain more confidence and boldness in who you are to accept the changes that have transformed them into who they are. You will learn something new about your spouse every day, so you have to commit to the relationship and allow God to show you the way.

Showing Godly love is the A.R.T that will allow you to communicate, compromise, and commit. It's the same love that God shows us each and every day that wakes us up, gives us brand new mercies, gives us another chance to get it right, and constantly forgives us. And that's the A.R.T. that will make every aspect of the marriage right! Communicating with God first to know what Actions to take, being willing to compromise and take responsibility for the vows that you've made, and being committed to the relationship and what God has ordained will create a marriage masterpiece that will stand the test of time and last a lifetime!

Chapter Six

"A.R.T. Activities to Build
Your Marriage Masterpiece"

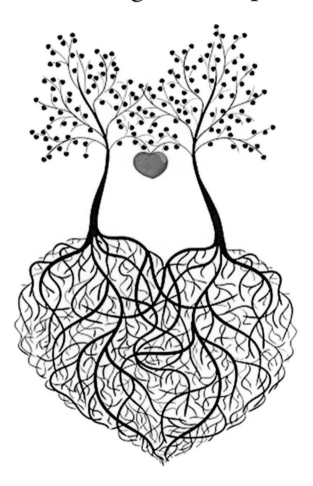

"A.R.T. Activities to Build Your Marriage Masterpiece"

Commitment is a work of A.R.T (Actions Responsibilities Time). To create your marriage masterpiece, you have to take the right action, be willing to take responsibility in and be responsible for your marriage, and take time to make time to work on your relationship every day. You want your marriage, so what are you willing to do to make it the masterpiece you want it to be?

Answer the questions and complete the activities to show your A.R.T commitments.

1. What can I do to show you that I love you?

Action

_____

_____

_____

Responsibility

_____

_____

_____

Time

_____

2. What can I do to be more helpful to you?

Action

_____

_____

_____

Responsibility

_____

_____

_____

Time

_____

3. What can I do to please you physically?

Action
_____
_____
_____

Responsibility
_____
_____
_____

Time
_____

4. What can I do to meet your needs emotionally and mentally?

Action
_____
_____
_____

Responsibility
_____
_____
_____

Time
_____

5. What's our dance?

_____

Are we dancing to the same beat?

_____

If so what (type) beat is it

_____

If not, what do we need to do get on the same beat?

_____

Action   _____

              _____

              _____

Responsibility _____

              _____

              _____

Time   _____

6. **What will we do to show that we Acknowledge, Accept, and Appreciate each other?**

Action

_____

_____

_____

Responsibility

_____

_____

_____

Time

_____

7. **What will we do to take A.C.T.I.O.N. (Actively Contributing to Touching, Intimacy, Oneness, & Needs) in our marriage?**

Action

_____

_____

_____

Responsibility

_____

_____

_____

Time

_____

8. How will we keep our commitments to our vows?

Action _____

_____

_____

Responsibility _____

_____

_____

_____

Time _____

9. What will we do to communicate better?

Action _____

_____

_____

Responsibility _____

_____

_____

_____

Time _____

10. What can we do differently to compromise in areas where we haven't been willing to in the past?

Action

_____

_____

_____

Responsibility

_____

_____

_____

Time

_____

A.R.T activities are essential to creating the right picture for you to understand the needs and desires of your spouse. Take ACTION daily to create the Masterpiece that you want your marriage to be!

Chapter Seven

"Testimonies"

"Testimonies"

Testimonies to make winning marriage!

Revelation 12:11 says, "They overcame him (Satan) by the blood of the Lamb and by the word of their testimony; and they loved not their lives unto the death" (KJV). As we face the battle with Satan in our marriage, the obstacles, and situations that come our way, we can face them with confidence and assurance that with Christ, we can and will be Victorious over all of them!

Everyone has a testimony. In marriage, as you allow God to lead the way, you will have something new to share with someone else and to celebrate every day. There are so many unique situations and circumstances that couples go through. You have your ups and your downs, good and bad, as well as times when you are happy or sad. Testimonies prove that *It's All About What You Make It* that allows you to overcome what seems to be impossible to take. God has given us the power to overcome evil and there's no weapon that's formed against us that can prosper. Negativity, evil, tough times, and complex situations will come; but with God they will not destroy you, they will only make you strong.

This chapter gives testimonies from couples that have chosen to make the best of their situations. Has it been easy? Of course not! But it has been "All about what they have made it"; continuously using the P.R.E.S.S, P.R.E.S.S., and the P.U.S.H (refer to Chapter 4) to make it the absolute best for their marriage to survive.

Testimony of Endurance!

In spite of what you go through, you have to always trust God. Every marriage vow that we've taken has been tested at some point throughout the many years of our marriage. When taking a look back, our issues were minor when compared to some people we know. Regardless of the magnitude of our problems, issues, or the people that have tried to ruin our marriage and our lives, God has always given us the power and the strength to overcome them and allowed our marriage to survive. We've endured a lot and had a lot to forgive and forget to keep our marriage together to this day. It has been a constant reminder to apply the Godly love that He shows us when he forgives us for all of our shortcomings; that has been our drive to stay together and go a little while longer. And no matter what we have gone through, we've been able to evaluate and cherish the valuable, incomparable things that he has given us in our children. And nothing that we've gone through has ever affected the morals and ethics that we've instilled in them. We've always agreed on how we will raise them, what we will teach them, and how we will discipline them. We've always taught them to treat others the way you want to be treated, and to love your neighbor as yourself. It's been by the grace of God that we've been able to sustain and overcome all that we have been through. Recognizing, respecting, and realizing that everything that God made is good, and it is He who made us and not we ourselves; therefore it's not our responsibility to try to change anyone. Accept, love, pray and allow God to have his way. Learn from your mistakes, forgive, and don't judge or hold grudges, and accept the things you cannot change, change the things you can. Accept God's wisdom and guidance to know the difference. Both of us have been stubborn. We've both tried to change the other. We've both lied at some point. We've both made mistakes and said and done things we've regretted. We both had family issues and history growing up that has affected us, how we feel, and how we respond. But what matters most, is that we both have had the determination and faith to trust God, love each other, and keep our marriage. There's more joy in being together than apart. There are happier memories of us together than apart. We can enjoy and celebrate our children and grandchildren better together than apart. There's more strength and stability in being together than apart. Being together continues to set the example for our children that we are willing to not just talk it, but we will press on to do everything that we have taught them.

A Testimony of Blended Success!!

As a couple who has had previous marriages, and this time around being blessed to have a blended marriage, we believe that there are several key things that must be present in order to have a successful blended marriage. Some of those things that we have identified are trust, communication, reassurance, prayer, and respect as key components. We have identified a few strategies that we believe will help to make a blended marriage work.

1. **Acceptance:** The couple must meet their spouse and children where they are and as they are. One cannot expect to change or unmold personality, character or behavior that has been shaped (or is shaping). They must accept everyone for who they are and assist them with where they want to go. You must expect a period of adjustment otherwise resentment may try to creep into your marriage. These adjustments include establishing new rituals and routines for the new residence as they will most likely differ from the previous family home.

Remember that this is a transition that requires patience. As a couple we have learned that it is more essential for us to meet the major needs of one another and the family even if it does not fit into the normal routine or schedule.

2. **Support:** The couple must continue to support the other at all cost. You must know that you may not always agree on how things are being handled, but you must lend your support to your spouse. The couple must accept their previous home structure in terms of discipline, approach to school and school works and recreational activities. While we are aware that the spouse may be new to the other, he or she is not new to rearing children and has already begun or deep into the formative process of shaping the children. It is not the job of the new spouse to rear or shape the children or offer opinions (especially unsolicited) about raising the children. It is the job of the new spouse to support the existing endeavors of the other spouse as it relates to the children with consequences and rewards. As a couple we have learned that we must support one another when it comes to all areas of raising the children. In a blended family you will have many different circumstances and tests that may arise, but if you lean, trust and depend on God, you and your spouse will make the right decisions.

3. **Modeling:** It is vitally important for the family

structure to model love and respect toward the new spouse and the children because it allows the children to see and set high expectations when they begin to date or eventually get married. The couple must model caring and kindness toward all, especially non-family. Children need to see how parents care for and respect each other with love. The couple should also model effective communication particularly when it is apparent to the children that spouses do not agree. We would say to NEVER raise your voice PERIOD. While the new spouse will get over it, one cannot discount the impact whether positive or negative that it may have upon the children. This could possibly set up resentment within the children because they may feel that their parent has been mistreated by this stranger. This is a key factor in effective communication. Screaming and yelling does not solve the problem, it only adds fuel, so when having intense fellowship to talk about situations just do it thoughtfully; you never know who is watching.

4. **Motherhood/Fatherhood:** Know the difference between being a "father/mother figure" and actually being the "father/mother". You must acknowledge that the children already have parents whom they love and cherish. Do not seek to replace, outdo, show up, or talk down about the other parent. During this process you must impose trust within

your spouse to know that they can and will make the right decisions in parenting. There are many times that you may want to offer your opinions about the father/mother's interaction with the children, but just know that you must continue to pray and trust your mate. As a blended family you must be available, accessible and focus on the needs of the children as well and the needs of your spouse.

5. **Commitment:** A blended family must always let their commitment show to one another and to the family as a whole. You must let the family see your commitment to God, and the importance of spirituality. The family must see the man as the head of the household and see his full commitment to follow God and ultimately lead your family into greatness. No it may not always line up with your emotions, but trust the God that is within your spouse to follow him as you follow God. The children must also see your commitment to your job/career. The family must model going to work, being and giving your best at work, taking your job seriously, but lastly that the job does not come before God and your family. The family should see a commitment to a life with purpose. The couple must model the difference between relaxation and laziness. When one is relaxing it is viewed as the reward for hard work, while laziness is the avoidance of work both spiritually and materially. The

blended family must ensure that their commitment to teaching their family that God will bless your family if you trust, believe, and are faithful to the gifts and talents that he has placed within your heart.

6. **Position:** The couple must put God first and foremost, and must model how the husband/wife must pray, follow God, trust God, and then make your decisions based on God's response. It is vitally important the couple prays for one another both openly and secretly each day and know that prayer does change things. The husband should model what a man should do in leading, praying and providing for the family. The husband must keep the family covered in prayer by acknowledging God in all of his ways and allowing God to direct their path. You must let your light shine before men that they might see your good works and glorify the father which is in heaven. We must remember that in our times of trouble, celebration, sickness, heath, fatigue, or rejuvenation we must bless the Lord. We must trust God during the hard times, the financial strains, the abundance, and the overflow. We must acknowledge that God is faithful to those that believe, so position yourself in prayer and supplication. Prayer can definitely change things!

Testimony of Determination:
No Distance Can Come Between Us!!

Yes, we can say with confidence that our marriage was meant to be. It took over 20 years for us to realize that our relationship was meant to go beyond a friendship. It's a true testament that God's thoughts are not our thoughts, and our ways are not His ways (Isaiah 55:8). From day one, distance has been the biggest challenge that we've faced in our marriage. We knew this would be the case, but we have been determined to trust God and allow him to show us the way. You would think that with the distance, trust would be a barrier, but it has only proven to us that we were meant to be together. Yes, it's hard! Yes, it gets lonely! However, when you are in love and you know that it is love......you do whatever it takes to make it easier. Face time, texting, and late nights on the phone are the cure for when we feel alone. But when we're both at home....it's on!! We make up for the days, the weeks, or sometimes a month that has gone by. We talk about our physical needs. We talk about our mental and emotional needs, and when it's time for those needs to be met, there is no hesitancy on either of our part. We continuously express our love with no limits, no boundaries, but with all our heart. So one mile or a million, it doesn't matter the amount; Our love for each other will always keep us close with no room for doubt.

A Testimony of Overcoming!

Genesis 2:24 reads "Therefore shall a man leave his father and mother, and shall cleave unto his wife: and they shall be one flesh" (KJV). Before anyone makes the decision to get married they must count the cost and look at the big picture which is Jesus. You will definitely encounter hills and valley's yet being in it together makes the ride much sweeter. Buckle up and understand the ride you are about to take.

Our marriage has been a testament to every vow we took on our wedding day. Our journey began on Saturday May 10, 2003 at 10:00 am when we said I do. That was the initiation of our bond together. We moved into our beautiful and new home that God had blessed us with, and began to conquer our challenges as Mr. and Mrs..... Every blissful and pleasurable moment that was experienced was tested by the hurdles that we needed to jump over, and the adversities we needed to go through.

The way we get through each test and work to overcome the challenges concerning our marriage would be to apply the Word of God, and to pray without ceasing. As a couple who desires to have a happy and fulfilling life together it is important to go to the Father in Prayer together, and on behalf of one another. It is important to touch and agree with one another as often as possible. When this takes place it gives power and authority to the husband and his wife. The bible says in Isaiah 54:17 *"No Weapon that is formed against thee shall prosper; and every tongue that shall rise against thee in judgment thou shalt condemn. This is the heritage of the servants of the Lord, and their righteousness is of me, saith the Lord"* (KJV). This should be spoken every time the enemy tries to rise against you or what your marriage represents. This is the way every husband and wife can pull together to tear down all strong holds. It works for us because it is a principle of God that we choose to apply daily. It is important to operate in unity and never depart from each other in anger.

The advice we have for couples that may be experiencing these same or similar situations or challenges would be to always apply the principles of GOD. Trust that there is nothing that God can't do, change, heal or fix. Matthew 7:7 reads "Ask, and it shall be given you; seek, and ye shall find; knock and it shall be opened unto you" (KJV). When your desire is to please God first, and then your mate and you operate with a pure heart, GOD will bless your marriage and allow it to be a testimony to you and to others in JESUS NAME AMEN!

<u>A New Testimony</u>

We've only been married for a few years and the test came early. We've been together for a while and really thought that we were ready to face all that life would bring our way together. But, the truth is, we never thought it would be this way. It has truly been a test in so many areas.

Challenges with the differences in how we were raised, our family values, and knowing and understanding what the word family means and how we will bring these differences on one accord to raise our own children so they are not affected by the same obstacles we've faced. A test of our faith was created by our job challenges. Facing times of little to no employment, struggling finances, and trying to figure out who's responsible. Too much time was spent on questioning ourselves, our relationship, our love, our faith in God, our abilities, our trust in each other. Simply put, we were at a place of not knowing what to do, but prayer changes things! The effectual fervent prayers of the righteous availeth much. We never knew what that really meant until we sincerely tried it. We started praying for ourselves, asking others to pray for us and with us, and praying together. Even in the midst of praying, the challenges still remained, and more challenges came. Working hard to make ends meet, family members not understanding why I'm holding on; trying to listen, but not listen; and keep my vow to leave and cleave. Both of our minds in a state of confusion, we were praying, but it didn't seem like God was answering, or that there was any resolution. We realized when you want God to move, you have to move. We were expecting a physical change, when ultimately we needed a mental and spiritual change. We changed how we communicated. We stopped looking at what we didn't have, and started thanking God for what we did have. We started caring for each other and showing

God that we wanted each other, we wanted our family, we wanted our marriage. We are different, we handle things and situations differently, we see things differently and do a lot of things differently, but for us, that's the way it's supposed to be. That's the way God designed for it to be. We acknowledged, accepted, and now appreciate OUR family! Things have started to change, we don't react/respond the same way about our situations as we did in the past; because now we know, trust God, believe God, allow God, expect God, and understand that this too shall pass. In a number of years, it's a new marriage. With faith in God, it's a new beginning!

Realizing Our Testimony

My husband and I have been together for a lot of years. We have a beautiful family and our children grew up not knowing anything about what it's like to want and not have, To ask and it not be given, or anything about "lack "or "not having" of any kind. We were both blessed to have great jobs that brought in sufficient income, more than enough for us to do whatever we liked, whenever we wanted to; we just had to take time out of our busy schedules to do it. Going to church, acknowledging God, tithing, and doing what we thought we needed to do to glorify God. We had it to give; we did not know what it was like to not be able to give. Living a life that people admired; getting and having what we needed was never a challenge. We had it all, we thought, there were no real issues. Our individual incomes were way more than most, so that's what we relied on. So it wasn't so bad as most would have taken it, when my husband lost his job. My income was still enough to sustain us, we continued on. Then things started to get crazy on my job, my mindset started to shift, and I realized I was missing "something". I wanted more. I began to think about a change. I had the tangible things that I wanted, but I was still missing "something". Being on my job, with the company in the state that it was in, was just not fulfilling that need. I began to pray and ask God for guidance and direction, and God answered. I resigned from my job. Even in the midst of this life-changing transition, my husband and I were very supportive of each other. We started a family business; and yes all praise and glory to God; because we couldn't believe it. It's easy to support each other and encourage each other as husband-and-wife, when things are going well and you can "see the light at the end of the tunnel". But when the light gets dim, when things started to get tough, not enough money for this/that, maxed out in ways that we were not accustomed to; our relationship started to change. Our tones were not the same, our support for and belief in each other was not the same.

When the light at the end of the tunnel goes completely out, the one thing you have to realize is, during tough times, is when you need each other the most.

That's when your light should shine more than ever, so

you can see Christ in each other. No, things may not be the way they used to be. Yes, some things you have to do without, but you don't have to do without each other. In the midst of struggle, trust like you never have before, love like you never have before, believe and have faith in God like you never have before. When tough times seem more than you can bear, know that God's grace is sufficient. You can endure the trial together. Allow it to make you stronger: For better, for worse, for richer, for poorer. Through it all, it has to be," until death do us part"!

Are things where we think they should be with our finances, with our business? No! But God! We know that we will overcome. Our faith has grown. Our love for each other has not gone, and our family has a new Psalm----"the Lord is my Shepherd, I shall not want". Realizing now that for so many years our thought process was all wrong.

We realize now that abundant life has nothing to do with your social status, your income, or how well you are living. Abundant life is your faith in God your faith in each other and most of all, the love, grace, and mercy that God keeps on giving.

A Testimony on Making It All Work

We started our marriage very young. Young love that has taken us on a journey far beyond what we could have ever imagined. A child, not our plan, but definitely God's will at hand, led to our wedding day; on an adventure that we knew God would have to lead the way. From day one, we placed God at the forefront. We used the example and foundation of our parents to get us through it; the initial ups and downs, bumps and bruises of a young couple, with a small family, and had no idea what we were doing. We held it together, by the grace of God; because by our own strength, we just could not do it. Challenges came, but our love remained. Then baby two and three appeared, and our lives truly made a change. The example that we had from our parents, we couldn't really use it anymore. With baby three, things were not the same! So Lord, what do we do now? We had to trust God and believe that he would see us through somehow. We developed our own routines, family vision, and traditions. Little did we know, there was much more in store. God blessed us both to work from home. Husband working – wife the home-maker. During the day, we were able to work some time in alone. We have always acknowledged, accepted, and ap-preciated our roles. We work hand in hand, talk things through, and make sure we don't step on each other's toes. There is never a dull moment. More challenges came; then dance, gymnastics, football, and baseball games. We established routines, we were making it all work, and then we received the news that we were pregnant again! Okay Lord, this can't be! We didn't have time for ourselves as it was; another baby? We had to trust God, pray, and allow him to tell us what do. Little did we know that it was not one other baby, but two! We never imagined having a family of five. We still have to pinch ourselves to see if we are dreaming. So how have we survived? With the 5 P's...

1. **Prayer**------ Our relationship with God went to another level when we got married. It's imperative to stand on God's word, trust, have faith, fast, and pray.

2. **Put aside our selfish ambitions**----------We had to learn to go with the flow and live each day one day at a time. We've had to put our individual agendas aside and adapt to the navigation of the family.

3. **Parent with a purpose**----------Our attention is focused on raising sane, saved, and secure children; raising them to be good, productive citizens. Of course we emphasize educational and career success, but top priority is being good, God-fearing, and followers of God's word.

4. **Parent playtime**------We make an intentional effort to spend time together as husband and wife. For example, every Friday we've set aside a couple of hours to make sure that it happens consistently.

5. **Partner with grandparents**-------It's important to us that our children spend time with our parents. This serves two purposes: 1. a bond with their grandparents that creates a lifetime of memories. 2. gives us the opportunity for more "parent playtime".

As you've read each of these testimonies, I'm sure there was something you could relate to, compare to, and even witness to. So look at your situation and know that your life is not too complex for God. Jesus controls the storms of life (Matt. 8:25) and every test and trial is only a passing storm that builds your testimony and makes your marriage stronger!

Chapter Eight

"Prayers"

"Prayers"

<u>A Prayer for Husbands and Wives</u>

God I pray for every husband and every wife individually and collectively. I thank you for blessing us with someone who cares for us, who wants to take care of us, and who's concerned about our happiness and well-being. Lord please allow your love and your peace in marriages, so that hearts and minds can align and be on one accord with your will and your way for the family. Touch the hearts of every husband so their love and desire for their wife and family will grow stronger and stronger, and their love and obedience will be so great that their every action will be to please you, Their love will be an example of you, and their vision and leadership within the home would be what you have ordained it to be. In the name of Jesus! Touch every wife that their love and desire will be to please you first and their husband and children will be pleased. Give wives a mindset of peace in prayer knowing that they can take every care and concern to you and you will care for the needs of the family, they will know what to say and exactly what to do. Amen.

A Prayer for Strength in Marriages

God strengthen marriages right now in the name of Jesus that couples will be prayed up to fight against the enemy that tries to destroy marriages. That husbands and wives will recognize when the enemy is trying to attack and they will call on you and pull closer and closer together and not allow anything or anyone to come between them or separate them from the love of God. We praise you! And give your name all the honor and glory. In Jesus name! Amen.

A Prayer for Confidence in Marriages

Heavenly father bless every couple within our circle of friends. Help us to pray for one another and encourage one another on this marriage journey. Help us to not judge, compare, or condemn each other. Prop us up on every leaning side that we will all line up and lean only to you for understanding of our relationships. Show us your way and give us the strength to follow you each and every day! In Jesus name! Amen

A Prayer of Humility

Lord so many times we don't understand why or how things happen in our marriage. Please give us clarity and a clear view of what we need to say and/or do. Help us to trust in you. Show us, teach us, and help us to do what you would have us to do; so we can be the husbands/wives you have ordained us to be. And our marriages will be all it needs to be to represent honor and glorify you. Amen

A Daily Prayer for My Wife

Lord I thank you because you have blessed me with this helpmate and partner. I ask that you would pour out your abundant blessings upon her. I pray for her as she goes about her day, give her peace and rest in all that she endeavors to do.

Please guide her as she makes decisions and she influences those with and outside of this family. Help me to love and cherish her in real and substantial ways, may she find me as a supporter and a friend. Keep her in your care today Lord, and encourage her with knowledge and your love. Touch the mind of my wife, the heart of my wife, the spirit of my wife! Strengthen her faith and trust in you so that she can be a faithful follower and believer in God first, and that her actions line up to your word to follow and trust the vision and leadership of her husband; And knowing that God will honor obedience and bless our household. Touch her mind so that even when she can't see the vision or understand the vision of her husband, that she will trust you and pray to you so that you can lead and direct her path and allow the vision that you have given to manifest in the name of Jesus! Amen!

A Daily Prayer for My Husband

Lord I thank you for my husband. I thank you for his heart and the love that he has for you and the love he has for our family. Please cover and keep him and allow your presence to surround him with your peace and your protection. May you give my husband his heart's desire and not withhold the request of his lips. Help my husband to excel in all that he puts his hands to. Fill him with the knowledge of your will in all spiritual wisdom and understanding, so that he may walk in a manner worthy of you to please you in all respects, bearing fruit in every good work, and increasing in the knowledge of you. Strengthen him; give him confidence, and may you bring victory to him in every place the sole of his foot treads. May the words of our mouth and the meditations of our heart be acceptable in your sight, O Lord, our strength and our redeemer. In Jesus name! Amen!

Prayer for Couples

Lord your word says in Ecclesiastes 4:9–11 *"that two are better than one because they have a good reward for their labor. For if they fall, the one will lift up his fellow, but woe* to him that is alone, when he falls he has not another to help him up. Again if two lie together, they have heat, but how can one be warm alone? And if one prevails against him, two shall withstand him and a threefold cord is not easily broken."(KJV) Lord help me to walk with my spouse, talk with my spouse, and live for you, so I can love my spouse. Help me to be forgiving so I can be forgiven. Strengthen my faith to trust you and allow you to take full control, and have your way! Please give us freedom in our marriage to love, to laugh, to live together in healing, Harmony, and happiness. In Jesus name! Amen! Amen! Amen!

The Word of God tells us to pray without ceasing. Therefore we have to be in constant prayer for our marriages. God will give us the strength that we need to put forth our very best as husbands and wives to glorify him in holy Matrimony; and stay together for better or worse, for richer or poorer, in sickness and in health, until death do us part. It's All About What You Make It, and with God you can make it the best together! *Wherefore they are no more twain, but one flesh. What therefore God hath joined together, let no man put asunder" (KJV). (Matt. 19:6).*

Applying It to Your Marriage!
Taking It To The Next Level

"Triple A" -Acknowledging, Accepting, and Appreciating
Read Matthew 20:11
Proverbs 3:5-6
Romans 5:8
Romans 8:28
Jeremiah 29:11

Two to Tango—Prayer, Partnership, and Protection
Genesis 2:18-24
Matthew 19:6
Ecclesiastes 4:9-12

T.A.G. You're It! ---Words, Work, Willingness!
Take it, Accept it, and Give it!
T—Telling your partner when you need help
A----Accepting how they help you and how they handle the situation
G-----Giving them credit for taking on a responsibility that is out of their comfort zone!

The Rules to T.A.G. You're It!

***Turn it <u>O.N.</u> (oppose the need) before your spouse gets <u>O.F.F.</u>
(Overwhelmed, frustrated, and fatigued)
***Be Reachable, Agreeable, and Teachable
***Plan, Prioritize, and Prepare

Take Time Out

Matthew 24:35 - 46
Make Every Moment Count!
It's not the quantity of time, it's the quality of the time
spent together that matters most!
Take time to make time to show your spouse that you
love them, you care, and you're there for them!

Take and Tell the Truth

John 8:32
2 Timothy 1:7-8
Hebrews 11:1-3
Romans 8:28
Philippians 3:13-15

P.R.E.S.S.	P.R.E.S.S.	P.U.S.H
• Please	• Pray	• Pray
• Recognize	• Recognize/Release	• Until
• Every	• Express Your Feelings	• Something
• Situation has a	• Seek God for an Answer	• Happens
• Solution	• Save Your Marriage	

The Truth/(Faith +Forgiveness)=Freedom

Test of Time

Commitment, Communication, Compromise

Hebrews 10:15-25

The A.R.T. of Commitment is

Action, Responsibility, Time

Take A.C.T.I.O.N

Actively Contribute to Touching, Intimacy, Oneness, Needs

References

(1) Life Application Study Bible, NIV, Tyndale House Publishers Inc. Notes and Bible Helps copyright 1988, 1989, 1990, 1991 by Tyndale House Publishers, Inc. New Testament Bible Helps copyright 1986 owned by assignment by Tyndale House Publishers, Inc.

(2) Tango: A Deeper Look; copyright Sharner Fabiano 2010. First published in the International Journal of Healing and Caring May 2010; volume 10 no. 2

Holy Bible, KJV (Broadman & Holman)

The Woman's Study Bible, Second Edition; copyright 1995 by Thomas Nelson, Inc.

The Love & Respect Experience- A Husband Friendly devotional that wives truly love written by Dr. Emerson Eggerichs

A daily prayer for husbands; Soul-mate; www.soulmate-film.com/newsletter/pdf/mwprayerpdf.

Chelle; Letters from the Heart; For My Wife; Heartfelt, Inc.2001 Salem, VA

Thank you!

We would like to thank God for this awesome opportunity to be a vessel to share the good news about marriage. We are so thankful for the journey that we've experienced in our marriage and want to share so much with couples everywhere that marriage is truly All About What You Make It and with God, you can make it the absolute best.

Special Thanks to:

Pastor Micheal Benton and First Lady Yvonne Benton
Nadira Benton
Ricky and Vivian Burney
Usher Consulting
Demond and Jessica Hammonds
Toney and Miriam Liggett
Mario and Nakia Norman
Benjamin and Robin Bryant
Stacey and Annetta Smith
Kerry and Sharlene Stroud
Indra Andrews
All of our family and friends for your prayers and support!